Faith, Love, & Narcissism

A Healing Memoir of Becoming Her

by Amiana Monik

Faith, Love & Narcissism: A Healing Memoir of Becoming Her

ISBN(Paperback): 979-8-218-65373-6

Cover and interior design by Amiana Monik

Printed in the United States of America

For inquiries or permissions, contact:
hello@amianamonik.com www.amianamonik.com

Library Of Congress Control Number 2025906661

Dedication

For every version of me who fought to get me here—
The little girl. The broken woman. The warrior in the
mirror. And for the healed version of me who finally
came home to herself.

This is an ode to your resiliency.

To the woman who's been through the fire and still
showed up soft.
To the ones who lost themselves trying to love others
whole.
To every silent prayer, whispered "yes," and sacred
boundary.

This is for you.

> With love,
> Amiana

Acknowledgments

To God—my anchor, my author, and the only reason I made it through. This book is nothing without Your grace and mercy and I am nothing without Your presence. Thank You for meeting me in the wilderness, in the silence, among the tears, and in the secret place.

To my children—Jachai, Jaylin, Dasan, and DaShae. You are my greatest callings, my daily reminders of legacy in motion. Watching you grow gave me the strength to rise. I pray these words help you see the power of healing and the beauty of becoming.

To my husband—Tim, thank you for being part of this journey, for your own growth, and for the space we've created through truth, redemption, and grace.

To my village—Especially my mom, Monik, and my grams, Margiree—your early support of my entrepreneurial journey, my dreams, even when it looked unconventional, helped me believe it was possible.

To everyone who saw the vision before it made sense, who prayed when I was too tired to speak, and who reminded me that I am worthy, even when I forgot.

Thank you for your belief. Your love. Your covering.

To every woman who's ever shrunk her essence to keep the environment comfortable, silenced her voice to keep the peace, questioned her value to feel chosen, or carried unwarranted weight she was never intended to bear—I wrote this with for you. Your story deserves tenderness. Your healing deserves honor. Your experience deserves a safe space.

And finally—to Amy. The younger me. You did not suffer in vain. You were never too much. Thank you for surviving, for believing, for holding on. I honor your tears, your bravery, and your fight.

With love,

Amiana

Table of Contents

AUTHOR'S NOTE

Some chapters in this book are long, others are brief. Just like life.

I used to feel frustrated about that—until I realized even the short chapters held weight.

This book reflects my becoming: the valleys, the peaks, and the pauses in between.

And through it all, I gave thanks.

For the healing, the clarity, the survival.

May these pages meet you in your own becoming and remind you—you're not alone.

Preface: I Got It From Here

The moment where I took the deepest sigh of relief and cried from the pit of my soul... It wasn't during a breakthrough.

It wasn't on a stage or in a therapist's office.

It was in my kitchen.

I was scrolling Instagram, watching video after video of soldiers coming home to surprise their families. The hugs, the tears, the reunions—the kind of videos that tug something loose in your chest even when you weren't expecting to feel anything.

And the song playing in the background of every single one?

Surrender by Natalie Taylor.

By the tenth video, it wasn't about them anymore.

It was about me.

About every version of me that had crawled, clawed, cried, and survived to get to that moment.

I put my phone down.

And without thinking, I wrapped my arms around myself.
I hugged myself.
Not out of pity. Not out of pain. But as a promise. A declaration.

"I got it from here."

It was like I was telling the little girl in me, the broken woman in me, and every silenced version in between:

I didn't abandon you. I didn't forget. I didn't give up.

We made it.

There was no blueprint for this. Just heartbreak... resilience... and a mustard seed.

The kind of faith that, from the outside looking in, would be labeled delusional. But I trusted God that much—that His word wouldn't come back void. Even for me.

I didn't write this book to be brave. I wrote it because I didn't want my silence to become my story. I needed to put language to the things I carried, the prayers I never said out loud, and the woman I almost didn't recognize anymore.

Every chapter in this book holds a piece of me I had to fight to reclaim. Some pages still sting. Others carry oil. All of them are honest.

This isn't a "tell-all." It's a heal-through. It's for the woman who has loved hard, lost herself, and is learning to rise like a phoenix—with softness still intact.

It's for the girl who was never too much. The wife who wonders if she's disappearing. The mother who's still trying to mother herself.

If you find yourself in these pages, know this—I see you. And even more than that... God sees you.

May this book meet you in truth, remind you of your worth, and call you back to yourself with grace and glory.

Let the healing begin

With love,

Amiana

Chapter One
The Prayers I Never Prayed Out Loud
Alexa, play In One Place by Tasha Cobbs Leonard

There are prayers I whispered in my spirit but never dared speak aloud. Not because I didn't believe God could handle them—but because I wasn't sure *I* could.

Some prayers were too heavy. Some, too honest. Others carried the kind of truth that would unravel everything I worked so hard to hold together.

So, I prayed in the quiet places. In the shower. In the car. In the pauses between the chaos. I never needed a pulpit to connect with God—He met me in rooms where my tears fell quietly, and my hands stayed busy holding everyone else together.

Faith, for me, wasn't just a belief. It was a lifeline. It was the reason I *didn't* lose my mind when circumstances tried to break me. His word never came back void, and even when life pressed in on every side, I knew—deep in my bones—that He would keep me.

This chapter isn't about a polished faith. This is about the kind of faith that carries you through silently, daily, and without applause.
The kind that stands firm—not because everything's perfect—but because God is still *God*.

I didn't go to Texas looking for a breakthrough. I was just there to surprise my friend Ashley for her birthday. But as I often do, I pulled up TikTok to find new places we could explore—and something about **Prayer Mountain** kept showing up on my feed—over and over. I felt this quiet tug in my spirit like; *you need to go there.*

So, we did.

We typed it into the GPS, got in the car, and started driving. We didn't know what to expect—neither of us had ever been there—but I knew I needed to be.

When we arrived, it was still. Beautiful. Covered in trees, blooming in silence. No crowds. Just nature, breath, and a peace I hadn't known I was craving. Only two other women were there.

Ashley and I walked up to the platform that overlooked trees stretching out into the distance. On the horizon—water, still and glimmering in the light of the setting sun. We stood there quietly, just taking it all in.

One of the women had been praying softly. She stopped and looked at me—not in a way that felt strange or intrusive, but in a way that said she saw *something*. She asked if she could speak to me, and I said yes.
She looked at me—not just with her eyes, but with something deeper. When she asked if she could speak what God was showing her, I nodded. Her voice was gentle but steady, like someone who knew she was just the vessel—not the author.
And then she said something that hit my soul in a place I didn't even know needed words:

2

"It's almost like you've been marinating for the right time," she said.

"God has had you marinating for such a time as this. Because many are going to eat of your fruit, and God has been infusing you with His anointing, with His glory like never before—so when you bear fruit, it's good for the consumption of nations."

I didn't know her. She didn't know me. But it was like she had a direct line to the conversations I'd had with God in the dark—when I questioned the wait, the warfare, and the weight of the call. And here she was, reminding me that I wasn't *behind*. I was being *prepared*.

Every delay wasn't denial—it was **divine marination**. Every moment of silence was seasoning. Every unseen act of obedience was part of the process to make sure what I carry *nourishes others, not just impresses them.*

I left Prayer Mountain differently. Not in the fall-on-your-face kind of way. But in a quiet, soul-settled kind of way. The kind of difference that doesn't announce itself but becomes obvious in how you carry your silence, your strength, and your surrender.

I didn't have all the answers when I walked away from that platform. But I had something better—*clarity*. I had been seen. Confirmed. Covered.

And that was enough.

From that moment forward, I stopped looking for big signs or loud affirmations. I realized God had always been speaking—I had just been too surrounded by noise to hear Him. My faith didn't grow because I witnessed a miracle. My faith grew because I remembered that *I* was one.

But mountaintop moments don't stop real life from showing up.

I came back home full—but life didn't care. The chaos hadn't paused while I was getting poured into. The laundry still needed folding. Kids still needed me. And the same issues I'd left behind were right there waiting, like they had been sitting in the living room sipping tea, unbothered.

It was jarring, to say the least.

Because how do you go from being told nations are waiting on you... to scrubbing dishes and stretching yourself thin to keep your household from falling apart? How do you hold onto the spiritual when the physical is screaming for your attention?

There were moments I wanted to return to that bench on the mountain. Just to feel seen again. Because when life is loud—when everyone needs something from you and there's nothing left to give—it's hard to remember you're chosen. It's hard to remember the prophecy when all you see is the pressure.

But this is where my faith lived—in the chaos. Not in the quiet.

It was easy to feel God on the mountain.

It took *intentionality* to feel Him in the middle of a messy kitchen, an argument I didn't have the strength to finish, and a version of me I was trying hard to hold together.

Faith, for me, was never about the absence of chaos. It was about finding clarity *in* it. It was about holding onto what God said—even when everything around me screamed the opposite.

That trip to Prayer Mountain didn't erase the weight I carried. But it reminded me I wasn't carrying it alone. It showed me that God doesn't just meet us in sanctuaries—He meets us in stillness, in surprise encounters, and yes, even in TikTok algorithms.
It's easy to celebrate the mountaintop moments. But I'm learning that the real beauty of faith is how it anchors you in the valleys.

And this—this was only the beginning.

"Yet God has made everything beautiful in its own time."

— Ecclesiastes 3:11

Reflection & Journaling

•   What are the prayers you've whispered in your spirit but never said aloud?

_____

_____

_____

_____

_____

•   Where has God met you in your most chaotic or ordinary spaces?

_____

_____

_____

_____

_____

•   Write a letter to yourself—one that acknowledges how far you've come even in the silence.

_____

_____

_____

_____

_____

_____

Chapter Two
The Tables Will Turn—But So Must My Heart

There's a difference between confirmation and conviction. Confirmation tells you, "You're on the right path." Conviction tells you, "But your heart needs checking before you get there."

When I left that mountain, it wasn't just the visions of favor and fruitfulness that stayed with me. It was the part that pierced deeper—the part that said, *"He's going to send them back."*

The ones who doubted.

The ones who talked.

The ones who disappeared when I needed their presence the most.

God said I would sow into *them.* That the same ones who withheld would one day need my overflow. And when they returned—not to apologize, but to witness—He asked me to keep my heart open.

Not for their sake.

But for mine.

The Word That Convicted Me

When she said it, I wanted to act like I didn't hear her right. I almost looked around like, *"Surely that part wasn't for me."* Because it wasn't the "nations are waiting" that stopped me in my tracks—it was what came after.

"Even those who doubted you... even those who talked about you... God said He's going to send them back. He has to. So, they can see the very thing they said wouldn't happen, is going to happen. And when He sends them back, keep an open heart... because you're going to sow into them."

Huh?

Not *bless* them.

Not *block* them.

Not *tell* them how bad they hurt me or make them apologize first.

No—God said I would **sow into them**.

I had to hold back laughter, tears, and a full-blown internal *protest*.

Because the truth is... that word didn't come as confirmation. It came as conviction. And it hit a nerve I didn't want touched.
I had *already* forgiven more than I wanted to. I had *already* extended grace where I could've pulled receipts. So to hear that *I* would be the one to pour into the same people who made me feel disposable?

Who doubted me, dismissed me, *and* made me question my worth?

That wasn't a word I shouted over.

That was a word I *wrestled* with.

I didn't say anything out loud at the time. I glanced at Ashley for a brief second, and with unspoken words she knew what didn't sit well with me. She knew my pain. My heartache. My experiences. I just nodded, smiled politely, and held my composure. But inside? I was flipping tables in the temple of my heart.

God... You want me to sow into the same people who planted doubt in me? The ones who couldn't clap when I was winning in silence? The ones who made me feel like my voice was too much, my dreams too big, or my presence too inconvenient?

Say sike right now.

And let's be real—I wasn't just hurt. I was *disappointed*. Deeply. Because I wasn't talking about strangers or seasonal people. I was talking about the ones *I* rooted for.
The ones I thought would be front row at my breakthrough—but instead, they were backstage, whispering.

And now You want me to pour into *them*? Really?

The Heart Check

I sat with that word for days. Not because I didn't believe it. But because I *knew* what it would require of me. It would require a **healed heart**. A **surrendered ego**. A level of grace that didn't come naturally to a woman who'd been betrayed publicly and clapped back privately.

I wasn't worried about the blessing.
I was worried about my heart posture.

Because blessings come easy when the heart is soft. But what do you do when yours is still riddled with scars?

But God doesn't just drop a word and leave you with it.
He *works* it into you—slowly, intentionally, and sometimes painfully.

And that's what He started doing with me. It didn't happen in a church service. It didn't happen in a moment of worship. It happened in the quiet—on regular days when I'd hear their names and feel my chest tighten. When I'd replay what they said, what they didn't say, how they exited without care—I would feel my heart drop and heat rise behind my eyes.

That's when I felt the gentle nudge of hard truth: "*You can't carry them and the calling at the same time.*"

And that was devastating.

Because I *thought* I had already released them. I *thought* I had already forgiven. I *thought* I was further along the emotional road of recovery than I truly was. But what I had really done was create *distance*, not *deliverance*. I had walked away, but I was still carrying what they left behind.

God started bringing them to mind—not to torment me, but to *tenderize* me.
And every time I resisted, I was reminded,
"*This is not about them. This is about your heart.*"

So, I prayed—not for their return, but for my readiness.
For the ability to hold favor and forgiveness in the same hand.
For the strength to smile and sow, even if their apology never came.

Evidence of Healing

I remember the first time I felt the shift.

I was in conversation with someone who knew us—nothing deep, just casual and friendly. They didn't know behind the scenes how things unfolded. Their names were brought up. I wasn't thinking about *them*.

I wasn't trying to speak on them. I was just... enjoying the conversation.

And then there I was left to give an answer on how they were doing. No trigger, no warning. And instead of tension, tears, or rehearsed comebacks... I said, "They are doing well."

That was evidence.

That was healing doing what healing does when you surrender it to God—quiet, steady work in the background of your heart.

And it wasn't just in conversations.

There was a day I came face-to-face with someone who had deeply hurt me—someone who had emotionally hurt my child. I didn't know I'd see them. There was no time to brace for it. **Years of silence. Absence. No explanation. And as far as I was concerned..no justification.**

And in that moment, all the things I thought I'd say— **every angry, *justified* word I had rehearsed in my head—**

I said none of them. Surprisingly, not even my face said what my heart at one point desired to say.

I turned around... and walked away

.

Not because I was weak. But because the healing journey had quieted something in me that no longer needed to scream to be heard.
That, too, was evidence.

It didn't mean I wanted to be close again.
It didn't mean trust would be restored. It didn't erase the pain or rewrite the past— but it proved
I was no longer tethered to it.
But what it did mean was *freedom* had entered the room.
And for the first time, I wasn't holding space for their wrongs—I was making room for my *growth*.

Healing isn't always loud.
Sometimes it slips in through the cracks—showing up in your tone, your posture, your peace.
Sometimes, healing looks like speaking well of people who wounded you, not because they changed—but because *you did*.

And sometimes, healing looks like saying nothing at all— not because you're weak but because you've grown strong enough to **choose silence over satisfaction**.

And that's the real assignment: to grow in grace, even when it costs your pride.
To be prepared for the return—not with bitterness, but with bold surrender.
To hold the blessing without becoming bitter.
The tables *will* turn.

But before they do... God is making sure my heart will too.

> **"Above all else, guard your heart, for everything you do flows from it."**
> **— Proverbs 4:23**

Reflection & Journaling

•   Who do you need to forgive—not for their sake, but for yours?

_____

_____

_____

_____

_____

_____

•   Are there areas in your heart still tethered to offense, disappointment, or unspoken grief?

_____

_____

_____

_____

_____

_____

• What would it look like to walk in your blessing without bitterness?

_____

_____

_____

_____

_____

_____

Chapter Three
When Forever Had Conditions
For the ones I never thought I'd lose. For the version of me that loved without limits.

It was the first time in my life I walked away from something. The first time I realized the abandonment wound was no longer holding me captive.

I used to think love was forever—especially with the ones I did life with. The ones I called family, best friend, sis.. you know the ride or dies. The ones I prayed for, built dreams beside, and assumed would be in *every* chapter of my story.

But it's one thing to cling to people out of love.
It's another thing to cling out fear of being left.
I saw forever in people who only saw me for a season.
And when the season changed, so did they.

They didn't leave loudly. Some just drifted.

Others... made choices that made it impossible for me to stay connected and still protect my peace.

And I won't lie—there are names I *still* hesitate to say out loud. Not because I'm bitter, but because the memory of loving them still deeply stings.
But the difference was **this** time, I let them go.

This isn't the kind of heartbreak people write songs about.

This is the *grief* of losing people who are still very much alive and well.

It's the ache of watching "forever" be forcefully defined as seasonal.
But even with letting them go, I was proud of myself for removing their access.

It hurt. It was one of the hardest things I'd ever done— because letting go didn't just leave me feeling disconnected. It left me in a season of isolation.

But it was in the season that God started refining me. It's where He started working on me, carving out the distractions that had been clouding my vision.

Sometimes, in order to level up, you have to strip away the things that keep you stagnant. And for me, that meant letting go of the ones I was convinced would always be there.

God wasn't just asking me to let go of them—He was asking me to trust Him. And asking me to make room for more.

What I didn't expect was that making room for more would start with making room for me.
It taught me that a **party of one** wasn't as terrifying as I had made it out to be.

I had spent so much time surrounding myself with people that I feared being alone would feel like punishment.

But while I was still learning to transition from going places as a group to going places alone, something shifted.

I was making space for myself when I thought I'd be making room for other people to fill that void.

The season of isolation forced me to be **my own friend before anyone else ever showed up**. And the more I embraced that, the more I realized I didn't need to wait for someone else's approval to live the life I wanted.

I started doing solo outings—dining alone, exploring new places, showing up for myself the way I used to show up for everyone else. What began as loneliness transformed into something else: **liberation**.

I discovered joy in my own company. And in doing so, I uncovered parts of me I had buried beneath other people's expectations.

What I didn't realize then was that **living out loud— embracing solo outings, reclaiming my joy, being unafraid to be seen on my own—was inspiring other women to do the same.**

Sometimes, making room for more means **learning how to stand alone first.**

God was stripping away the distractions, the noise, and even the people who no longer fit where I was going. What felt like isolation was really **preparation**. He was showing me that growth doesn't always require an audience.

It took being alone to realize my value wasn't tied to who stayed, who left, or who decided I was worth the effort.

I wasn't waiting for other people to see me anymore—I had learned to see myself.

And when you learn to see yourself, you stop shrinking to fit into spaces you've outgrown.

This season wasn't just about releasing others. It was about releasing the parts of me that still needed outside validation to feel worthy.

And as I stepped into this new season of solitude, I realized God wasn't calling me to a place of emptiness.

He was calling me to a place of fullness—fullness of His presence, fullness of purpose, and fullness of me.

I wasn't missing anything. I was becoming everything I was always meant to be.
The isolation I feared so much had turned into a gift.
It stripped away the noise, the distractions, and even the people who no longer fit where I was going.

It taught me to cherish my own company, to celebrate my own growth, and to walk boldly in the truth of who I am.

And for the first time, I wasn't running from isolation. I was walking confidently through it.

"Letting go doesn't mean I stopped caring. It means I choose peace over picking up pieces.

Reflection & Journaling

• Who was your "forever" that turned out to be temporary?

_____

_____

_____

_____

_____

• In what ways have you mourned someone still alive—and how has that shaped your understanding of grief?

_____

_____

_____

_____

_____

• Write a goodbye letter to a friendship or relationship that you've had to release in love.

_____

_____

_____

_____

_____

_____

Chapter Four
This Ain't What I Prayed For

There's a moment in every woman's life when reality and prayer collide. When the very thing she once called a blessing starts to feel like a burden. And she has to ask herself, "Did I miss God... or did I settle and call it Him?"

I prayed for love.
For legacy, for covering, for something rooted in heaven and grounded in truth.
But the truth is—I didn't always know how to receive what I was asking for.
Because I was still healing from a blueprint of love that was flawed.

And somewhere along the way, I started confusing endurance with love.
Silence with peace.
Sacrifice with strength.
I started shrinking in rooms I was meant to stand tall in—just to keep things together.

It wasn't about blame.
It was about awakening.
About realizing that the version of love I was holding...
wasn't what I prayed for.

I kept telling myself it was just a rough patch. That if I prayed harder, showed up more, gave more grace, stayed quiet longer... it would pass.

I called it *covering*. I called it *submission*. I called it *strength*.

But deep down?
It was survival.

I was surviving something I never thought I'd have to survive in the context of love.
And the hardest part was that from the outside, it didn't look broken.
There was no scandal. No betrayal.
At least not *yet*.

But when it came... when the truth surfaced and I saw what had been hidden behind charm and comfort... it didn't just hurt.

It *wrecked* me.

Spoon-fed lies.
Heart wrenching betrayal.
The realization that what I was holding onto so tightly was never built on truth.

But even then, I prayed.
Even then, I stayed.

Because I was still clinging to the promise... even though the foundation had already cracked.

I had prayed for love.
But I was managing dysfunction.
And I had to be honest with myself:
This wasn't what I prayed for.

This wasn't what God promised.

The truth is...
I accepted things in the name of love that I knew were dysfunctional.
But because they looked familiar, they didn't feel alarming.
They felt *normal*.

I wasn't ignoring red flags.
I was recognizing them as part of a pattern I had learned to call love.

Because the *original blueprint* I had for what love from a man should look like?
Was *flawed*.

It included silence instead of safety.
Control instead of covering.
Discomfort dressed up as sacrifice.
And the idea that being *chosen* was enough—even if being *cherished* was missing.

So, when I found myself in a relationship that mirrored what I'd seen growing up...

I didn't call it toxic.
I called it *tough*.
I didn't call it harmful.
I called it *hard work*.

Because that's what I *believed* love was supposed to be:
Earned. Endured. Justified.
Even if it cost me *me*.

I used to think I knew what love looked like. But the truth is—I only knew what it looked like to *need* love.
To perform for it. To prove I was worthy of it. To chase it, cling to it, and convince it to stay.

That wasn't love.
That was a reflection of **abandonment** I hadn't yet named.
A root planted early. Quietly.
Long before I had language for the ache.

I didn't see it clearly until I started asking myself why I stayed so long in something that was slowly breaking me.

And the answer wasn't "because I'm strong."
It was "because this felt *familiar*."

Because when the **blueprint is broken**, you start to think survival is strength.

You start to believe that enduring silence, manipulation, emotional distance, or inconsistency is just part of love's test.

I didn't realize how many of my standards were shaped by what I *didn't* receive as a child.
By what I was afraid to lose.

By the belief that if I could just love someone hard enough, maybe they'd finally choose to stay.

So, I tolerated *too* much.
Forgave *too* quickly.
Explained things away that should have *never* happened.
Gave myself away to people who **never** deserved that intimate space.
Accepting moments of *feeling* chosen.
While *desperately* looking for a love that would stay.

Not because I didn't value myself, but because I was searching for connection in places love was never meant to live.

But because **I was still carrying a broken blueprint in one hand and my heart in the other.**

And one of the hardest truths I had to face was the disappointment I carried from the first man in my life.

The man who was supposed to be my first true safe space— my first protector, my first example.
He was my first love and my first heartbreak.
As I grew and began to trace the root of my wounds,
I found abandonment quietly tucked beneath our memories.

The kind that doesn't show up in loud exits, but in silent absences.

How do you forgive someone who never acknowledged the pain they caused
Or accepted the responsibility of placing me on the wrong trajectory?
How do you heal when the apology still to this day has never been presented?

Still, I kept navigating life.
Kept healing.
Kept peeling back the layers.

Because what was more important than your children?
Your firstborn daughter.. all of your daughters?

And what about your son?
The one who should've been taught what it meant to lead with love, not wounds.

The one who **deserved** to be shown how to be a man by a man-- not left to navigate the silence in private.

The one who shouldn't have had to explain why he needed his father.
Or wondered if asking was asking for too much.

But I would be the one who could no longer hold it in.
The one who bled the silence into sentences and turned pain into pages.
Because it wasn't just me.
We were *all* carrying questions.

All of us deserved something more.

And at some point, even the quietest ones start to ache out loud.

That truth hit something in me I hadn't fully named yet.
We were worthy of love that prioritized us.
Not performance.
Not image.
Not silence.
What could possibly matter more than preparing your children for the kind of love you hoped they'd one day receive?

Rewriting the blueprint didn't happen all at once.
It came in fragments.
In journal entries, in therapeutic sessions, in quiet cries to God when no one else knew I was breaking.

It came after asking myself hard questions and sitting in answers I didn't want to face.

Answers like:
I had spent years trying to be enough for people who were never taught how to hold someone like me. I had tried to prove I was worthy of staying when it was never my job to beg someone not to leave. I had to learn that love isn't meant to be *earned*.

That I don't have to *prove* my worth to be chosen.
That someone staying isn't always a blessing—and someone leaving isn't always a loss.

I had to **unlearn** the idea that love has to hurt before it heals.
That "struggle love" was a part of *everyone's* love story.
That self-sacrifice is the cost of connection.
That I was created to carry everyone else's needs while silencing my own.

I had to start choosing myself. Not
in a selfish way, but in a sacred
way.

The kind of choosing that says,
"I will no longer abandon myself to keep anyone else."

And it was in that choosing... that God started to
rebuild me. Not all at once.
But year after year of celibacy.
Piece by piece.
With truth, with grace, and with the kind of love I
had tried to earn from everyone else— and finally
realized I could only receive from Him.

In the stillness.
In the surrender.
In the sacrifice.
In the moments I stopped performing for love and
started receiving it.

God didn't just mend what was broken.
He revealed what was buried.

The parts of me I had hidden beneath survival,
beneath "being strong,"
beneath the fear that if I showed up fully, I'd
be too much to love and too hard to keep.

And when I finally faced all of that—laid bare under
the weight of what I'd been carrying— I knew I
couldn't just pray about it.
I had to start healing through it.

So, I did something that surprised even me... I became
my own first client.
I didn't enroll in Life Coaching and NLP courses just
to help other people.
I enrolled because I was trying not to lose my mind.

I needed something that would help me make sense of the space I had found myself in— the unraveling, the silent screaming, the version of me holding everything

together while feeling like everything inside me was falling apart.

I'd look in the mirror and see the woman everyone called strong.
A strong Black woman.
But even the strongest deserved softness. Even she needed the space to unravel without shame.

I had worn resilience like armor, convincing myself that holding it all together was the only way to survive.
Strength had become both my weapon and my prison.

I had mastered the art of smiling through pain, of lifting others even when I felt like I was sinking. But strength alone was not enough—because strength without healing is just survival.

And I was exhausted.

I realized I had been surviving on strength alone for so long, that I had forgotten softness was also mine to claim.

I had trusted spaces where I could release my heaviness without judgment— but even then, the weight of it felt like mine alone to carry.

I had always known that strength and vulnerability could coexist.
But I was learning that healing required me to stop performing wholeness and start seeking it.

Prayer has always been my foundation.
It's still more than enough.
But as a millennial woman of faith, I've also come to understand that healing is layered.
Faith and therapy. Prayer and processing. The divine and the deeply human.
I needed both—because the unraveling needed room to breathe, and the healing needed permission to begin.

I grew up hearing "what happens in our house stays in our house."
But silence was eating me alive.

And while I tried to be quiet about the circumstances, on the inside, I was screaming— trying to undo the truth that the mask had fallen, the beautiful box was empty, and I was still trying to be the glue when I felt like dust.

Those certifications didn't just teach me tools for others.

They didn't just give me the credentials to be seen as an asset.
They helped me navigate back to myself. They helped me remember that **faith without works is dead.**
I was still carrying the mustard seed— but now I was learning an added layer to fight with it.

Healing wasn't just about what I believed God could do—
it was about what I was willing to confront, uncover, and rebuild with Him beside me.

The certifications weren't *just* about gaining credentials.
They required me to sit with my own patterns, excavate my own pain, and become my own first client.
They challenged my mind— while
God continued to heal my heart.

I didn't ask for the pain.
But the healing?

That part was both learned and received.
That part was answered prayer.

**"I'm no longer abandoning myself for the sake of connection.
Whoever stays, must love me whole."**

Reflection & Journaling

•   Where did your original blueprint for love and worth come from—and how has it shaped the way you show up in relationships today??

_____

_____

_____

_____

_____

•   Write a letter to your younger self. Speak to the version of you that craved love, validation, or presence from someone who didn't know how to give it. Tell her what she deserved then—and what you now choose for her moving forward

_____

_____

_____

_____

_____

•Where in your life are you still abandoning yourself to keep someone else comfortable? And what would sacred alignment look like in that space instead?

_____

_____

_____

_____

_____

• What would it look like to rebuild your definition of love—from a healed place?

_____

_____

_____

_____

_____

_____

Chapter Five
The Charmer & The Mask

*A slow unraveling of charm that covered
control, and the moment I realized love was
being weaponized.*

They don't start with cruelty and emotional dismissal.
They start with charm.

They start with the right words, the right tone, the
right attention in all the places you've been neglected.
They mirror your dreams. Study your softness. They
learn your love language and speak it *fluently*— until
it becomes a currency of control.

That's how the mask works.
It's not *what* they say that reveals them. It's what
they *do* after they believe they've secured your
trust.

I didn't fall for a cruel and heartless monster.
I fell for a version of him I believed in...
A version of someone that seemed safe. Stable. Sent.

But what I didn't realize...
was that I had entered a quiet war with someone who
mistook the rare for the replaceable.

A diamond in his hand— still searching for cubic zirconia's.
Only seeing what I could offer, not who I *truly* was.
Shaping me beneath the weight of his calculated control.

It didn't fall apart all at once.
It unraveled—slowly. Quietly. Internally.
Before anything changed on the outside... *I did.*

I started second-guessing myself.
Started shrinking mid-sentence.
Started apologizing for things I hadn't even done, just to keep the peace I wasn't even feeling.

I was in a constant state of emotional negotiation.
Balancing his moods. Starving mine.
Making space for *his* version of truth while quietly burying my own.

It wasn't screaming matches or reenactments of WWE's Monday Night Raw
It was silence used as punishment.
It was emotional distance followed by just enough affection to keep me hopeful.
It was being made to feel overdramatic for expressing needs, and ungrateful for naming my pain.

It was mental gymnastics dressed in concern.

It was manipulation wrapped in "miscommunication."
It was me unraveling... and him pretending he didn't notice.
It was a calm storm that slowly but surely would leave debris of damage like a violent tornado.

And still—I called it love.
Because I didn't have language for what it really was...
Not yet.

Self-doubt became my closest friend. Not because I didn't know who I was— but because I kept being told I was "too much" and "not enough" at the same time.

One minute I was praised. The next, I was picked apart.
One moment I was everything *he* wanted.
The next... amnesia would come in like a thief in the night.

It was the slow erosion of my certainty.
The quiet way I started questioning my own instincts.
The way I stopped trusting my gut—not because it was wrong, but because *he said it was.*

And that self-doubt?
Didn't just live in the relationship.
It followed me into rooms I was *called* to be in.
Into platforms I had *prayed* for.
Into blessings I *earned.*

Suddenly I was shrinking on stages I had built.
Questioning compliments.
Overexplaining my success.
Over apologizing for even the smallest things.

Wrestling with imposter syndrome—not because I
wasn't qualified, but because somewhere along the
way, I was made to believe that I couldn't trust myself.

I didn't just lose confidence.
I started fearing my own reflection.

Because if someone who claimed to love me could
invalidate me so easily, what if everyone else was just
pretending too?

That's what emotional manipulation does. It
doesn't just make you doubt *them*... It
makes you doubt *you*.

Something shifted the day I chose to stop sending
subliminal messages on social media, hoping he'd see
them. To stop blasting songs like You Got Me Waiting
by Fantasia, thinking the lyrics would speak for me. I
made the decision to lock in and *starve the
distractions*.

I decided to reclaim my energy, my mind, and my
voice. But reclaiming my energy didn't start by
deleting posts or cutting ties. It started with *feeding
myself* reminders of empowerment. It started with
sermons and affirmations—like Girl Get Up
by Sarah Jakes Roberts—

42

that spoke to the woman I was becoming, not the pain
I was nursing.

Reclaiming my mind didn't start with shutting down
all the noise—the voices that swore I was failing, that
life was over, the **taunting**...

It started with a *tattooed semicolon*, a permanent
reminder that it gets greater later if I persevere.

Reclaiming my voice didn't start with shouting to be
heard.
It started with tears and whispers.
It was me writing truths in my journal that I was too
ashamed to say out loud.

It was praying those prayers that didn't ask God to fix
him, but to restore *me*.
Because I wanted my marriage. I wanted my family.
My children deserved the kind of upbringing I didn't
get the chance to have– a two-parent household.

But somewhere in that longing, I also realized...
I deserved a love that didn't hurt.   I, too,
deserved more than the shadows. I deserved to
be loved out loud–
to stand beside, not behind someone else's pain,
To be the rib God crafted me to be.

It was looking in the mirror and learning how to hear
my own voice again—without adjusting it for his
comfortability.

At first, it felt uncomfortable.
My voice shook with every "no."

I second-guessed every word. Every boundary.
Because I had spent so long making myself small, I
forgot **I was never created to shrink**.

But little by little, I started choosing me.
I started believing in myself again.
I started trusting the sound of my own thoughts
without needing them to be validated or filtered.

**I stopped apologizing for being direct. Stopped
dressing up my emotions so they'd be easier to
swallow.**
**Stopped handing my peace over to people who
treated my softness like weakness.**

My voice didn't come back all at once.
It rose—like breath.
Like freedom.
Like a phoenix rising from ashes.

And when it did...

I realized **I was never too much**.
I had just been in environments that wanted less of
me than I was designed to give.

The dynamic didn't shift on its own.
It took everything *completely* falling apart.

44

It took undeniable truth breaking through illusion. It took me finally **unclenching my grasp**... and God finally stepping in.

Because I had tried to fix it in my strength.
I had tried to endure it with my silence. But when I found myself of the brink of depletion emotionally, spiritually, and mentally— I realized: *this wasn't just a breakdown. It was an intervention.*

God didn't just remove the mask.
He *removed* the access **completely**.
Not even the spirit of narcissism could stay in proximity when God started doing what only He could do.

And here's the plot twist I didn't expect:
While *I* was healing... *he* was being stripped too.

God was dealing with us *both*.
Separately.
Individually.
Intentionally.

Because transformation doesn't always happen in comfort.
Sometimes it happens in collapse.

It took rock bottom to realize performance, pain, or pride was never meant to last.
If anything sacred was going to rise from this... it had to be *orchestrated by God **alone***.

So, this time, I'm not rebuilding by default.

I'm rebuilding by *design*.
And only what's in alignment with truth, healing, and vulnerability gets to stay.

Redemption didn't come wrapped in a pretty box with a precisely placed bow.
It came in therapy sessions, quiet prayers, uncomfortable conversations, and raw openness.

It came in **accountability**. In **apologies accompanied by action**. In **growth** I never thought I'd see.
Not just in me—but in him, too.

Because while I was healing my heart, *he was confronting his own reflection*.

God wasn't just restoring me—He was refining *him*.

Making the choice of accepting that childhood environments and trauma would no longer be an acceptable scapegoat to remain stagnant.

The choice of learned toxic behavior would no longer be the truth lived but the lie dismantled.

An intentional choice of stepping into the destined-filled position of breaking generational curses—

Allowing God to be his navigating compass, his anchor.

And no, it didn't erase the damage.

It didn't undo the years of pain or rewrite the past.

But it gave both of us a new blueprint— One where love is no longer held hostage by ego, silence, or survival.

People romanticize redemption, but they rarely talk about the labor of it. The courage it takes to stay while the other is still healing.

Most don't make it that far. They love the idea of restoration— until they meet the cost.

It might've been easier to just walk away. Because if I'm honest? I never made reconciliation a cakewalk.

But there he stood. Willing to fight. To rebuild. To restore. Not perfectly. Not always gracefully. But consistently. And that fight? It mattered.

This isn't a fairytale ending.
This is *redemptive unfolding*.
We're still becoming.

Still unlearning.
Still building something new from the wreckage of what almost destroyed us.

And the difference now?
It's rooted in *truth*.

And where truth lives, the mask can't stay.

**"See, I am doing a new thing!
Now it springs up; do you not perceive it?
I am making a way in the wilderness and
streams in the wasteland."
— Isaiah 43:19**

Reflection & Journaling

• Have you ever questioned your voice, your worth, or your instincts because of someone else's manipulation? What truths about yourself are you reclaiming now?

_____

_____

_____

_____

_____

• List 3 ways you're learning to trust yourself again.

_____

_____

_____

_____

_____

• Write down one boundary you now honor that would
  have protected the earlier version of you.

_____

_____

_____

_____

_____

_____

Chapter Six
Soft Doesn't Mean Stupid

*A return to softness. A reclaiming of self-love.
A reminder that my boundaries don't make
me bitter—they make me better.*

For a long time, I thought softness was something I
had to earn back.
Like it was a luxury only the *healed* version of me
could afford.
But the truth is—softness was never the problem. It
was the people who tried to take advantage of it that
made me question it.

I wasn't weak.
I was *wide open*.
I wasn't stupid.
I was *unprotected*.

And when you've been mishandled, misread, and
manipulated long enough... you start to believe that
armor is your only option. But God didn't call me to
be hard—He called me to be *whole*.

So, I started the slow, sacred journey back to myself.
Through boundaries.
Through self-care.
Through intentional time set aside for just me and
Jehovah Ropha.

Softness, I realized, isn't the absence of strength. It's the presence of *security*.

It's loving yourself loud and long enough that no one else gets to define what worthiness looks like for you.

Self-care wasn't bubble baths, shopping sprees, and skincare routines.
At first, it was hard.
It was awkward.
It was me sitting in silence, realizing just how much I had poured into other people leaving my reservoir empty.

It was canceling plans without guilt.
It was saying no as a full and complete sentence. It was looking in the mirror and reminding myself that I didn't need to shrink to keep peace.

I didn't wake up one day suddenly admiring the mirror's reflection.
It was a *journey*.
A decision I made—*daily*—to choose myself without waiting for permission.

Self-love looked like:
- Writing affirmations even when I didn't believe them yet
- Buying myself flowers without needing a reason
- Going on solo dates and enjoying my own company

- Intentionally rebuilding my environment
  back into feeling like a safe haven instead of a
  prison

It was in those quiet moments—when the world didn't need me, and I finally needed me—that I started to heal from the inside out.
Because somewhere along the way, I realized:
Softness isn't about being delicate.
It's about being deeply aligned with who I am, what I need, and what I refuse to tolerate ever again.

I wasn't always available anymore.
Not because I stopped caring, but because I started *prioritizing*.

And for some, my distance felt like betrayal. But what they didn't understand was—*this version of me didn't leave them.*
She just finally came back home to *herself.*

Some fell off quietly.
Others got loud and offended.

But I kept showing up for me.
Because anyone who sees your softness as defiance was never honoring your soul to begin with. And anyone who only loved you when you were broken— was never
loving *you.*
They were loving your *brokenness.*

So yes, I lost people.

But I also found *peace*.
And I'll **never** trade that again.

I used to think I had to harden to protect myself. But now I know—I don't have to become cold to stay covered.
I can be soft *and* strong.
Gentle *and* grounded.
Loving *and* discerning.
Because **my softness is not a weakness.**
It's a sign that I survived and *still* chose to feel.

Affirmation:

**"I am soft, worthy, and no longer shrinking.
My love is intentional.
My boundaries are divine.
And I am no longer afraid to be full of
everything God made me to be."**

Reflection & Journaling

• What lies have you believed about softness and strength?

_____

_____

_____

_____

_____

_____

• Where have you been overextending yourself in the name of love or loyalty?

_____

_____

_____

_____

_____

_____

- Who are you becoming now that you're no longer shrinking?

_____

_____

_____

_____

_____

_____

Chapter Seven
I'm Not Going Back There
Alexa, play I Won't Go Back by William McDowell

I've seen too much now.
Heard too much.
Healed too much.
Grown too much.

There's no version of me that can go back to the places, the patterns, or the people that required me to abandon myself just to belong.

God didn't bring me through the breaking, the healing, and the revelation for me to return to what made me question His voice in the first place.

So, no—I'm not going back there.

Not to performing.

Not to over-explaining.

Not to carrying relationships by myself.

Not to spiritual confusion disguised as submission.

I didn't just leave some places.
I was *delivered* from them.

And you don't go back to what God had to break you free from.
Not even for closure.
Not even for comfort.
Not even for company.

Because peace is expensive.
And I *paid* for mine in tears, truth, and therapy.

Freedom doesn't always feel like fireworks.
Sometimes it feels like waking up and realizing you're not anxious anymore.
Like answering the phone without your stomach turning.
Like smiling for real, not just for the picture.

Freedom feels like reclaiming your mornings.
Your energy.
Your mirror.
Your voice.

It's no longer rehearsing what to say to make someone else comfortable with your growth. It's not second-guessing your boundaries or explaining your peace.
It's walking into a room and not shrinking—because you finally believe you belong there.

Freedom isn't loud.
It's steady.
It's sacred.
And for me, it's personal.

Because when you've lived under the weight of performance, people-pleasing, and pain disguised as purpose...

Being free feels like a *revolution*.

And no—I'm not going back there.
Not even in memory.
Not even in imagination.
Not when I know what it feels like to be whole.

I don't need closure.
I don't need approval.
I don't need anyone to understand the version of me that had to walk away to survive.

I am free.
And that freedom was fought for, prayed over, cried through, and covered by grace.

I'm not going back to the pain I prayed to escape. I'm not returning to the silence that tried to swallow me.

I have tasted peace.

I have embraced purpose.

I have chosen myself—with God at the center.

And no matter what comes next...
I'm not going back there.

Reflection & Journaling

•   What patterns, people, or places are you being
called to release for good?

_____

_____

_____

_____

_____

•   Write a declaration beginning with "I'm not going
back to..." and list every mindset or situation that no longer
aligns with your healing.

_____

_____

_____

_____

_____

- How does peace feel in your body? Describe what freedom looks and sounds like in this season of your life.

_____

_____

_____

_____

_____

_____

Chapter Eight
Called, Not Just Chosen
Alexa, play Reckless Love by Israel Houghton

Being chosen felt good.
Being celebrated. Affirmed. Seen.
I got used to the claps, the "you're so strong," the way people leaned in when I spoke.

But being *called*?
That's different.
That's **cost**.
That's waking up to the realization that this story—*my story*—was **never** just for me.

Being called meant I had to go through it publicly and privately.
Called meant the weight hit different.
Called meant I couldn't just *post through it*—I had to *pray through it*.
I couldn't just *talk* about healing—I had to *live it out loud*.

And here's what I've learned:

You can be chosen and *still* be hiding.
You can be anointed and *still* be in survival mode.
But when God *calls* you?

He starts stripping everything that doesn't align with the assignment.

I remember the moment.
It wasn't some huge conference or altar call. It was years ago—at a quiet workshop on how to write a book.

At the time, I was just starting.
Starting to craft. Starting to blog.
Pampered Luxe wasn't even called Pampered Luxe yet—it was Pampered Love.

And even though I wasn't fully walking in anything yet... I felt *something* stirring.
After the session ended, a woman came up to me.
She didn't ask my name. She didn't ask what I did.
She just looked at me with a calm certainty and said:
"You're going to define your own lane. The gift is in your hands."

And I froze a little.
Because I *knew* she meant more than just books.
More than blogs. More than body butter.

She was *confirming* what I didn't yet have language for.
That I was called.
That something in me was going to shift atmospheres, stir hearts, and build something that had never existed before.

And even though I didn't fully understand what it meant...

I believed her without a doubt.

Because when you're called, you don't always need clarity— you just need a *yes* in your spirit.

Saying yes to the call didn't make things clearer.
If anything—it made things *messier*.
I questioned myself.
A lot.
One day I was confident. Inspired. Sure.
The next, I was second-guessing everything.
Was I *really* the one for this?
Did I even have what it takes?
Who did I think *I* was, trying to define my own lane?

There were days I wanted to quit—before I even got started.
I would talk myself out of posting. Out of writing. Out of showing up—because I was afraid of being *seen*.
That's the thing nobody tells you about being called:
You don't get to hide anymore.
God *will* keep pulling you out of every shadow you try to crawl back into.

Because this call?
It's not about perfection.
It's about obedience.

It's about saying yes even while trembling.

64

It's about showing up even while healing.
It's about doing it scared but still doing it.

And the more I said yes... the more the gift started
making room for me. And not just in rooms with other
people— but in the room I used to lock myself out of.
The one where I was *finally* allowed to take up space.

The more I leaned into the calling, the more I
realized *it was never about being "ready."* It was
about being *willing*.

Willing to keep writing, even when no one clapped.
Willing to create, even when I felt overlooked.
Willing to speak, even when my voice shook. Willing
to build what didn't exist yet—because I was called
to *birth* it.

And slowly, my life started to align.
Pampered Luxe wasn't just a brand.
It became a reflection of the woman I was becoming—
luxurious, healing, soft, and deeply rooted in truth.

My writing wasn't just therapeutic anymore.
It became a weapon.
A testimony.
A mirror for other women walking through their own
"what is this even for?" seasons.
Every time I chose purpose over fear; God
met me there.

Every time I chose to stay consistent with what He gave me— even in silence—He gave me confirmation without applause.

This wasn't just a calling.
It was a mantle.
And I had to carry it with intention.
Not perfectly—but *authentically*.

Because this time...
I know what's in my hands.
And I'm not letting anyone, including me, talk me out of it again.

I was never meant to fit in— I was called to build what didn't exist. I will no longer shrink for comfort. I will no longer second-guess what God has confirmed. I am not just chosen to be seen— I am called to shake the room. So I say yes. Yes to the weight. Yes to the work. Yes to the becoming. This time... I'm walking in it *for real*.

Reflection & Journaling

•   What's the difference between being celebrated and being called in your life? Where have you mistaken applause for purpose?

_____

_____

_____

_____

_____

•   What gift has God placed in your hands that you're being invited to carry with more intention?

_____

_____

_____

_____

_____

_____

_____

- Write a prayer or affirmation committing to your assignment—even if it costs comfort.

_____

_____

_____

_____

_____

Chapter Nine
She Built From the Rubble
Alexa, play No Ordinary Worship by Kelontae Gavin

I didn't start from stability.
I started from pieces.
Scattered moments. Broken seasons.
Dreams interrupted by disappointments, by detours,
by pain I never asked for.

There was no blueprint.
No perfect timing.
No clean foundation.

Just *me*.

Standing in the rubble of everything that didn't work,
everything that hurt, everything I thought I needed—
and deciding to build *anyway*.

Because at some point, I realized:
God wasn't waiting to bless the version of me that had
it all together.
He was waiting for the version that was *willing* to
build from what was *left*.

I used what I had:
A mustard seed of faith.

A bleeding heart.
A weary "yes."

And slowly— purpose rose
from pain.
Beauty rose from ashes.
And the woman I was becoming?
She didn't need perfect conditions.
She just needed *permission* to rise.

I built my peace from the pieces.
I built my identity from what was left after isolation.
I built my voice from silence.
My boundaries from betrayal.
My confidence from prayers that only God heard.

Pampered Luxe wasn't born in a boardroom. It was
born in moments when I had nothing left to give—
but still felt called to create.
It came from needing something soft to hold while the
world felt heavy.
From understanding that luxury isn't just in the
product—*it's in the pause.*
The rest.
The ritual.
The reclaiming of worth, one intentional moment at a
time.

Motherhood didn't pause the building—it sharpened
it.
Every "Mommy, I need you" while I was tired. Every
moment I poured out without having enough in me.
It showed me what endurance looked like in real-time.

But it also showed me what *legacy* feels like.

I built faith from moments that almost took me out.
Love from places that tried to bury me in loneliness.

And influence?
That came *after* the breaking— when I stopped trying
to be perfect and started being *present*.

Nothing I've built was handed to me.

It was fought for.

Cried through.

Pieced together in prayer and persistence.

And that's why I protect it now.
Because **I remember the rubble**.
And I remember what it cost me to rise.

I don't take credit for the strength.
I just honor the process.
Because what I built didn't come from comfort—it
came from collapse. And still... I rose.

I created.
I healed.
I grew.
Not because the odds were in my favor, but because
God *was*.

So when they ask how I did it, I don't boast—I remember.
I remember the rubble.
The heartbreak.
The nights I didn't think I had it in me.

The days I kept going anyway.

Because the truth is, I wasn't just building a brand, or a business, or a platform.
I was building **me**.

And now that I've laid this foundation in faith,
I refuse to let anyone make me question the value of what I've built.

Reflection & Journaling

• What areas of your life have you had to rebuild from the rubble?

_____

_____

_____

_____

_____

• How have your detours shaped your current direction?

_____

_____

_____

_____

_____

• Where have you seen beauty rise from ashes in your
  story?

_____

_____

_____

_____

_____

_____

• Make a list of everything you've built (within yourself or
  around you) that didn't come from ease—but came from
  endurance.

_____

_____

_____

_____

_____

_____

Chapter Ten
The Oil Is The Evidence

Alexa, play Alabaster Box by CeCe Winans

They see the glow now.
The platform.
The creativity.
The voice.

But what they don't always see— is the **crushing**
that produced the oil.

This influence wasn't manufactured.
It was *refined*—in private.
In silence.
In suffering.
In surrender.

Because legacy doesn't start on the stage. It starts
in the decisions no one claps for.
In the obedience no one sees.
In the moments when you could've stayed down—but
you got up *anyway*.

The oil on my life isn't just symbolic.
It's *evidence*.

Evidence that I kept showing up even when I felt
unqualified.

Evidence that I kept pouring, even when I was empty.
Evidence that I let God prune what I wanted to keep—
so He could trust me with what would last.

This isn't just impact.
It's an inheritance.
Because everything I've been through,
everything I've healed from, everything
I've built— It doesn't stop with me.
It *starts* with me.

Legacy isn't something I'm waiting to leave behind.
It's something I'm living out loud—every day.

It's in the way I show up for my children.
The love they receive without begging.
The emotional safety they don't have to earn. The
way they see softness and strength coexisting
under one roof.

It's in Pampered Luxe— not just in the products, but
in the intention. The way I remind women they don't
have to be falling apart to finally put themselves first.
The way luxury becomes a form of healing.
A ministry of touch, of care, of worthiness.

It's in my words.
The ones I used to hide.

The ones I write now with boldness, honesty, and oil.
The ones that remind others they are not alone—and
they are not too late.

This is the legacy.

It's not built on perfection.
It's built on permission.
To be whole. To be soft. To be called. To be seen.

And it starts with me.

I am not just building for now— I am
building for what comes after me.

My story is not just survival.
It is strategy.
It is blueprint.
It is legacy.

The oil on my life is not accidental.
It is earned through obedience, refined through fire,
and protected by grace.

I am raising legacy in my home.
Birthing purpose in my brand.
Shifting atmospheres with my voice.
And creating space for others to rise.
This influence?
It's not for clout.
It's for the Kingdom.

And I will steward it with reverence.

**Because the oil... is evidence that the crushing
wasn't in vain.**

Reflection & Journaling

• What "crushing" moments in your life have produced the greatest strength or wisdom in you?

_____

_____

_____

_____

_____

• How have your private sacrifices shaped your public story?

_____

_____

_____

_____

_____

- What legacy are you building right now—intentionally or unintentionally?

_____

_____

_____

_____

_____

_____

- Where do you feel God is refining you for something greater?

_____

_____

_____

_____

_____

_____

Chapter Eleven
It's Bigger Than Me

Because this assignment is generational. This obedience is breaking chains. And this voice— it's setting people free.

There are moments when I sit with everything I've written... everything I've walked through... everything I've survived— and I realize:

This was never just about me.

Not the pain. Not the
platforms. Not the
healing.
Not even the glow.

This was always about the ones coming behind me.
The woman reading this who doesn't yet believe she'll make it.
The daughter watching how I rise after the breaking.
The strangers who don't know my name but will find freedom through my testimony.

It's bigger than the brand. Bigger than the story.
Bigger than the applause.

This is legacy work.
This is ministry in motion.

This is what happens when healing becomes harvest.

When your yes starts setting other people free.
There was a moment when it hit me—*really* hit me.
That this... this voice, this healing, this journey I've
been on— was
going to reach people I might never see face to face.

And the weight of that?
It wasn't light.

It felt like sitting in a quiet room after sharing my
story and realizing the silence wasn't rejection—it was
reverence.
It was women messaging me like,
"I didn't know how much I needed that."
"You put words to something I couldn't explain."
"I thought I was the only one."

And in that moment, I felt it:
This isn't about content.
This is about *freedom*.

This is why I couldn't quit.
Why I couldn't hide.
Why I couldn't water it down or dress it up.

Because someone's breakthrough was locked inside of
my obedience.

And while the weight felt heavy at times— it
was also humbling.
Because *me* God? You sure?

Yes, even me...

When God trusts you with influence, He's really trusting you with *people*.

And I don't take that lightly.

Leading doesn't mean you always know what you're doing.
It means you show up—*anyway*.

It means hearing from God and still wrestling with fear.
It means creating space for others while learning how to hold space for yourself.
It means pouring out, even on days when you're running on fumes.
Not because you're trying to impress anyone— but because you understand that leadership is *sacrifice*.

Leading means going first... into the healing, into the hard conversations, into the becoming— so that someone else can walk through the door you had to *break open*.

It's not about the mic or the moment.
It's about the mantle.

It's making peace with being misunderstood.
Choosing depth over applause.
Faith over fear.

Obedience over popularity.

And most of all— it's trusting God to carry you *while* you carry others.

Because leadership?
It's not loud.
It's *purposed*.

The bigger the platform got, the
more I had to stay low.

Not low in confidence— low in
posture.
Low in ego.
Low in *need for validation*.

Because I've seen what happens when people rise
faster than they root.
When influence outpaces character.
When giftedness carries you where discipline can't
keep you.
So I made a choice:
To stay grounded in *who* I am and *Whose* I am.

To stay anchored in prayer.
To rest, even when the world rewards hustle.
To retreat when needed.

To stay sensitive to the Holy Spirit—even in rooms that want strategy more than surrender.

Because I never want to be so busy serving everyone else that I forget to sit at His feet.

My grounding isn't just what keeps me sane— it's what keeps me *whole*.

And if I ever feel the weight pulling me too high, too fast, too far—
I go back to the secret place.

Back to the stillness.

Back to the truth.

Back to the altar where all of this started.

Because I didn't build this life on ambition.
I built it on *alignment*.

I don't take the oil lightly.
I don't carry the weight casually. And I
don't serve for applause—I serve from
assignments.

I will lead with humility.
I will create with intention.
I will stay grounded in truth—even when elevation comes.

I'm not chasing platforms.

I'm preserving legacy.

And as God continues to expand what's in my hands, I
will stay at His feet.
Rooted. Ready. *Real.*

Because I don't just want to be used by God— I
want to be *trusted* by Him.

Reflection & Journaling

•   When did you realize your journey was about more than just you?

_____

_____

_____

_____

_____

•   Who is watching you become—and how does that impact the way you move?

_____

_____

_____

_____

_____

- What does "legacy work" look like in your life today?

_____

_____

_____

_____

_____

_____

Chapter Twelve
Compassion In The Face Of Betrayal

Some betrayals don't come from enemies. They come from people who stood beside you in sacred moments,
who clapped at your wedding, smiled in your photos, and called you "family."

I told myself I'd never look at them the same again—
How could they help cover the very wounds I was bleeding from?
I thought they were one of my safe spaces.
Because I wasn't just grieving what they did— I was grieving who I thought they were.

I had let them into sacred places in my life.
I had defended them. Laughed with them.
More than ten years of skin in the game. And in return, they handed my pain a pillow and told it to make itself comfortable.

I didn't need revenge.
I just needed distance.
I needed to protect the version of me that was still learning to trust her *own* voice again.
And I kept that distance... **until the day the phone rang**.
They were in the hospital.

Critical.
Unresponsive.

The doctors weren't sure they would make it through
the night.

And I froze.
Not because I didn't care— but because
I *did*.

There was a war in me: the part that remembered
their betrayal and the part that still remembered
how to pray for them anyway.
Because somewhere inside me, love hadn't completely
left— it had just learned how to guard its door.

I didn't go up there to reconcile. I
didn't go to prove anything. I went
because the healed version of me was
stronger than the hurt one.

**Yet walking into that room felt like stepping
into shark-infested waters.**
Their friends were circled together—whispering, side
eying, asking why *I* was even there.
My presence was questioned.
But, I didn't come for comfort.
I didn't come for *them*. I
came because, despite it all, *I
still cared*.

I had a right to be there, maybe even more than the ones who questioned *me*.

So, I stood at their bedside.
And I prayed.

Not because everything was okay— but because I was choosing to extend compassion while not becoming what had wounded me.

And I couldn't help but wonder...
Was this one of the very moments that lady spoke about at Prayer Mountain?
When she said they would come back.
When she said I would be tested—not in rage, but in *response.*
Was this the kind of return that wasn't about reconciliation, but about revelation?

Because this time, I *didn't* fold.
I *didn't* perform.
I *didn't* beg or lash out or shrink.

I showed up.
Soft-hearted.
Spirit-led.
Rooted in a kind of grace that couldn't be faked.

Maybe this was the proof.
That healing was taking hold.

That my heart was finding its *proper* posture—
one hand extending in compassion, the other
still guarding the door with wisdom.

I didn't leave the hospital with closure.

I didn't walk away with everything suddenly made
right.
But I walked away with peace.
Not the kind that comes from fixing what was broken,
but the kind that comes from knowing you didn't let
the devastation change *you*.

And maybe that's what grace looks like sometimes—
not forgetting, not excusing, but choosing to show up
differently because of who you are *now* and the
healing God has done *in* you.

This wasn't about being the bigger person.
It was about being the healed one.

Even if the apology never comes.
Even if the relationship never goes back.
You still get to walk away whole.

Reflection & Journaling

What has grace looked like for you when it wasn't easy to give?

_____

_____

_____

_____

_____

_____

•   Have you ever shown up for someone who deeply hurt you? What did that moment reveal about your growth?

_____

_____

_____

_____

_____

_____

•   How do you know when your heart is in a healed
posture—and not just a hardened one?

_____

_____

_____

_____

_____

•   Write about a time when you extended compassion,
not because they deserved it, but because you had changed.
What did that cost you, and what did it give back to you?

_____

_____

_____

_____

_____

Chapter Thirteen

Me, God, and The Monitors

Alexa, play Waging War by CeCe Winans

I had never felt more alone— and never been
more certain that I wasn't.

In 2020, the world stood still.
But in a sterile NICU room, mine kept spinning.
Monitors beeping. Nurses pacing. Prayers being
whispered like oxygen.
I had just given birth to premature 28 week old twins,
and nothing could have prepared me for what those
97 days would hold.

I couldn't rely on my mama this time—**my prayer
warrior**, **my anchor**—because the pandemic
stopped her from being *physically* present at the
hospital.
It was just me and God in that room. **And while
my twins were fighting for their place in
the world,
I was fighting for their covering.**

Not with noise.
But with presence.
With praise.
With prayer that would stretch my spirit and faith in
ways nothing else ever had.

They called it care.
But every diagnosis they tried to place on my babies felt like another arrow aimed at my peace.
First, it was Rickets.
Then, Pompe disease.
Then a list of complications and "what-ifs" that had me walking out of one storm and straight into another.

It wasn't just medical—it was mental. It was emotional.
And it became spiritual.

Because while the nurses charted symptoms, I was covering my children in scripture.
While they reviewed labs, I was praying for victory over tiny bodies.
While machines hummed, I was walking back and forth in that NICU, declaring life when death tried to whisper otherwise.

And when one of my sons had to go into surgery, I unraveled in ways I never had.
He was so small. So delicate. And I couldn't go with him.
I had never experienced one of my children going under like that—through gasps of breaths, a heavy heart, and tears streaming down my face... I was still anchored in a faith big enough to trust that **God would go where I couldn't.**

It wasn't the doctors I leaned on. It wasn't
the physical comfort of family— because
even that wasn't available.
It was me and God.
Me and the Word that **couldn't come back void.**
Me and praise and worship echoing through sterile
walls.
Me standing in the middle of a battlefield most people
couldn't see— but heaven could.

Because sometimes, you don't get to *choose* the fight.
But you can choose the *atmosphere.*

So I set it.

Over incubators.
Under dim lights.
In whispered lullabies that doubled as declarations.

I sang over them.
Not just to soothe—but to **cover.**
I laid hands when no one else was around. Not
because I had all the answers—
but because **I refused to let fear be the loudest
voice in the room**.

I watched feeding tubes go in.
I watched monitors spike and dip. I watched
time slow down and stretch out in unfamiliar
ways.
And yet—**I also watched God show up.**

Every milestone.
Every false diagnosis reversed.
Every breath they weren't expected to take... **they took**.
Because God was already there before I ever walked through those hospital doors.

And when we finally came home— after 97 long, faith-building, nerve-wracking days— I
wasn't the same mother who walked in.

I had been *carried*, too.

Reflection & Journaling

•   When have you found yourself in a battle that no one else could fight but you—and God?

_____

_____

_____

_____

_____

•   What did you learn about your own strength in a season where you had to cover others while barely holding yourself together?

_____

_____

_____

_____

_____

•   Describe a moment where worship became your weapon. What did it shift—internally or externally?

_____

_____

_____

_____

_____

•   Where in your life did God carry you in silence, and only now are you realizing just how deeply He was present?

_____

_____

_____

_____

_____

Chapter Fourteen
Unapologetically Her
Alexa, play I Made It by Fantasia feat Tye Tribbett

I used to walk into rooms and wonder if I was too much...
Now?
I walk in and wonder if the room is ready.

Because this version of me— the healed me, the whole me, the soft-yet-solid,
prayed-up, purpose-walking me— *she's not hiding anymore.*

No more shrinking.
No more dimming my light to make others feel comfortable in their shadows.
No more folding in half just to be liked, accepted, or tolerated.

I've done the work.

I've faced the wounds.

I've carried the weight.
And now... I walk in *wisdom.*

I've earned the right to show up as her— fully expressed, deeply grounded, and finally free from the need to be palatable.

Because the truth is, I was never too much. They were just never prepared for the version of me that didn't need permission to exist.

This version of me?
She prioritizes peace over performance.
Softness over survival.
Purpose over popularity.

She doesn't chase—she *attracts*.

She doesn't beg—she *becomes*.

She doesn't prove—she *protects*.

She no longer feels guilty for resting.
No longer over-explains.
No longer sits at tables where silence is safer than honesty.

She laughs more.
Lingers in her joy longer.
Takes up space—not to be seen, but because she finally sees *herself*.

She prays differently.
Creates differently.
Loves differently.

And not just romantically—she loves herself like she used to beg others to.

This version of me is not for everyone.
She doesn't have to be.

Because she's not performing anymore.
She's *present*.

And finally... she knows:
Unapologetic isn't loud. It's liberated.

I didn't arrive here by accident.
I *fought* for this version of me.
I cried for her. Prayed for her. Bled for her.
And now that she's here—
I refuse to apologize for her anymore.

Because everything I thought disqualified me... God used to develop me.

The heartbreak? Taught me grace.
The silence? Taught me to listen.
The betrayal? Taught me boundaries.
The wilderness? Taught me worship.

And now—
I'm not performing for love.
I *am* love.
I'm not waiting for permission.

I *am* the permission.
I'm not explaining my worth.
I *am* the evidence.

I've walked through fire, and I don't smell like smoke.
I've been made to bend, but I didn't break.

I've been stretched, but I didn't snap.
I didn't lose myself—I *found* her.

Every scar, every tear, every moment I thought would break me—**it all refined me like gold**. The woman I've become didn't happen by coincidence; she ascended from the ashes, molded by the heat and pressure of life life-ing.

As I continue forward, I'm not just *surviving*—I'm **thriving**.

I'm not just healing—I'm whole.

I'm not just existing—I'm living.

Gold by Joseph Solomon describes it best—how beauty rises from brokenness, how resilience glimmers after the darkest nights.

Thank God I don't look what I been through.
I am gold. And I'm walking away from this chapter—unapologetically her.

Final Declaration:

I am her.
Healed.
Whole.
Authentic.
And *completely* unapologetic about it.
This is my voice. This is
my truth.
This is my legacy.
And this time?
I own every word of it.

Reflection & Journaling

- Who is the most unapologetic version of you? What does she sound like, move like, believe?

_____

_____

_____

_____

_____

- In what areas are you still dimming your light or playing small?

_____

_____

_____

_____

_____

• What would it look like to walk fully in your truth—
  unfiltered, unshrinking, and unafraid?

_____

_____

_____

_____

_____

• What are you no longer apologizing for?

_____

_____

_____

_____

_____

About the Author

Amiana is a writer, speaker, creative, and multi-passionate woman of faith who believes in the power of healing out loud. As a mother, entrepreneur, and voice of resilience, she has spent years turning her pain into purpose—inviting women to see themselves in her story and remember the strength of their own.

She is the founder of Pampered Luxe, a brand that merges luxury with intentional self-care, helping women honor their worth through healing rituals and divine rest. Whether she's writing, creating, or simply holding space for others, her mission is clear: to help women rise, reclaim their softness, and walk in truth—unapologetically.

Faith, Love & Narcissism: A Healing Memoir of Becoming Her is her debut memoir and a testimony to what happens when you stop surviving and start becoming.

She's still healing. Still unfolding. Still becoming. And she invites you to do the same.

Connect with Me

This story may be finished, but the journey continues, and I'd love to stay connected with you.

Follow along for more healing, soft life inspiration, behind-the-scenes moments, and everything in between:

Instagram: @amianamonik

Instagram (Brand): @pamperedluxe

Website: www.amianamonik.com

Email: hello@amianamonik.com

Whether this book sat on your nightstand or stayed close in your heart– I'm grateful it found you. Thank you for reading.
Thank you for becoming.
Let's keep healing out loud... together.

With love,
Amiana